CELEBRATING THE CITY OF HOUSTON

Celebrating the City of Houston

Walter the Educator

Silent King Books

Copyright © 2024 by Walter the Educator

All rights reserved. No part of this book may be reproduced in any manner whatsoever without written per- mission except in the case of brief quotations embodied in critical articles and reviews.

First Printing, 2024

Disclaimer

This book is a literary work; the story is not about specific persons, locations, situations, and/or circumstances unless mentioned in a historical context. Any resemblance to real persons, locations, situations, and/or circumstances is coincidental. This book is for entertainment and informational purposes only. The author and publisher offer this information without warranties expressed or implied. No matter the grounds, neither the author nor the publisher will be accountable for any losses, injuries, or other damages caused by the reader's use of this book. The use of this book acknowledges an understanding and acceptance of this disclaimer.

Celebrating the City of Houston is a little collectible souvenir book that belongs to the Celebrating Cities Book Series by Walter the Educator. Collect them all and more books at WaltertheEducator.com

USE THE EXTRA SPACE TO TAKE NOTES AND DOCUMENT YOUR MEMORIES

HOUSTON

In the heart where bayous wend their way,

Celebrating the City of Houston

Houston sprawls, a realm where dreams hold sway.

A canvas vast where cultures blend,

From dawn's embrace to twilight's end.

Skyscrapers pierce the azure sky,

Reflecting hope as days go by.

Within these towers, stories spun,

Each tale as bright as morning sun.

The bustling streets, a vibrant vein,

Where voices hum a sweet refrain.

From Montrose art to Heights' embrace,

Celebrating the City of
Houston

Each district holds a unique grace.

In shadows cast by oaks so grand,

The echoes of a soulful band.

Jazz notes rise in twilight air,

A symphony beyond compare.

The Space City, reaching high,

Where astronauts and rockets fly.

A gateway to the stars we seek,

In Houston's heart, our spirits speak.

The bustling Port, a lifeblood stream,

Celebrating the City of
Houston

Fulfilling many a merchant's dream.

Ships laden with their worldly wares,

Converge where commerce never dares.

Beneath the surface, hidden gems,

In museums, theaters, diadems.

Art and science, side by side,

In Houston's arms, they both abide.

Cuisine that tempts from every land,

In Houston's kitchens, flavors grand.

From taco trucks to gourmet feasts,

Celebrating the City of Houston

A fusion where the palate meets.

The rodeo's call, a festive cheer,

Where cowboys brave and crowds endear.

Hats and boots and twang of song,

In Houston's soul, we all belong.

The parks, a green and tranquil space,

Where runners find a steady pace.

Memorial's path and Hermann's trees,

A refuge where the mind finds ease.

ABOUT THE CREATOR

Walter the Educator is one of the pseudonyms for Walter Anderson. Formally educated in Chemistry, Business, and Education, he is an educator, an author, a diverse entrepreneur, and he is the son of a disabled war veteran. "Walter the Educator" shares his time between educating and creating. He holds interests and owns several creative projects that entertain, enlighten, enhance, and educate, hoping to inspire and motivate you. Follow, find new works, and stay up to date with Walter the Educator™

at WaltertheEducator.com

www.ingramcontent.com/pod-product-compliance
Lightning Source LLC
LaVergne TN
LVHW012050070526
838201LV00082B/3898